FAKE MALE

THE REALITY OF SOCIETY

BAPI CHOWDHURY

Dedicated to all my mentors, a majority of whom remain unaware of my existence.

Acknowledgements

I would like to acknowledge the contributions of several individuals who have helped and motivated me to start and finish this book. First and foremost, I want to thank my parents for providing me with a comfortable life, which has enabled me to pursue this book. Often, we forget to appreciate the contributions of our parents, without whom we would be nothing. I also want to recognize the contributions of my teachers, who have consistently encouraged and motivated me to explore new things in my life. Additionally, I want to acknowledge the friends who have motivated me to write this book. However, the most significant contribution that I want to acknowledge is that of the people in our society. Their behaviour, characteristics, personality, and psychology have motivated me to unveil their true selves.

Preface

"Real man-made by the situation, not by themselves."

As a business management student, I have gathered some valuable experiences from my real-life encounters that I am sharing in this book. The aim of this book is not to teach you how to get rich or narrate some fascinating stories. Rather, I am writing this book to share my observations as an observer of life, I have keenly observed the personalities surrounding me and have drawn conclusions about them. One particular personality trait that has intrigued me is the tendency of some males to be fake.

In today's world, some individuals try to portray themselves as something they are not. As an observer, I have noticed a particular type of fake male who tries to pass off as an Alpha, a leader, or someone who has it all. These individuals use some psychological tricks and tools to appear superior in a group setting. However, I have developed the ability to detect these tricks and tactics and expose them for who thcy truly are- not superior.

In this book, I aim to highlight the main differences between various male personalities. You can use this knowledge to discover who you are and identify individuals who try to pretend to be someone else. It is not just about identifying these fake personalities but also learning how to deal with them, break them, and ultimately improve your personality.

Throughout the book, I will discuss the **11 rules** of fake males that they use as their primary tool. By detecting these personality traits, you can protect yourself from people who try to take advantage of you.

This book is all about this fake male or you can say fake man. Common humans can't identify them because they use some tricks very smartly, without knowledge about their characteristics we can't identify them in this crowded world. They are in front of us dominating us but we are following them blindly. someone says that **blinds show the way of blinds**. They are fake. If we do not identify them then It will harm not only us but also our society. So now let us discuss how to identify this kind of person who has a self-made personality or a "fake male".

This book is not solely about male personalities but also about human personalities who try to deceive you by pretending to be someone else. So, let us begin our journey of identifying fake personalities and learn how to detect fakeness that tries to rule over you.

All the examples I have used to establish the law are based on my real-life experiences. For privacy concerns, I have used some names that are not related to real people, but the events that have occurred are fully real.

"The real man smiles in trouble, gathers strength from distress, and grows brave by reflection."

CHAPTER I

Law of Fake Image

"The erosion of authenticity happens when a fake image creates an illusion. In this situation, reality is hidden by a facade, and truth is replaced by perception."

I. Introduction

Imagine scrolling through your social media feed, and your eyes are drawn to pictures of people living seemingly perfect and enviable lives. They are posing in exotic locations, wearing designer clothes, and boasting about their achievements. You can't help but feel a twinge of envy as you scroll through these seemingly flawless images. But what if I told you that these carefully curated images hide a dark truth?

Meet Sumi, one of my classmates from college. On social media, she projects an image of success, sophistication, and superiority. Each post and photo is meticulously curated to project a "perfect life." However, in reality, those who know her personally see a completely different side. She is annoying and lacks substance. Her attempts to portray herself as someone she's not are painfully transparent to those who interact with her in real life.

Sumi belongs to the category of what I call "fake pretenders," individuals who are masters of manipulating the "Law of Fake Image." They create false narratives about themselves, using social media to showcase a life that exists only in their imagination. Although they may fool some with their charade, those who are privy to the truth can see through their facade with ease.

Spotting fakes like Sumi is crucial because it helps us avoid disappointment and frustration. It also helps us recognize the damaging effects of living in a world where authenticity is sacrificed for social validation. By learning to see beyond the smoke and mirrors, we can distinguish between genuine connections and superficial facades.

In this chapter, we will delve deeper into the "Law of Fake Image" and explore how individuals like Sumi use it to manipulate perceptions and wield influence. We will uncover the telltale signs of fake image projection and equip ourselves with the tools to navigate the treacherous waters of social interaction with clarity and confidence.

So, get ready to take a journey into the heart of fakery, where we will learn to distinguish between real and fake. With knowledge and insight, we can emerge unscathed on the other side, ready to take on the world with clarity and confidence.

II. Unmasking the Fakers

Now that we've peeled back the layers of deception surrounding individuals like Sumi, it's time to delve deeper into the twisted game they play. At the core of their manipulative tactics lies the "Law of Fake Image" – a sinister force that thrives on falsehoods and fabrications.

But what exactly is this law, and how does it operate? Allow me to shed some light on the subject.

The "Law of Fake Image" is the unwritten code by which fake individuals operate. It's a playbook filled with strategies and tactics designed to create and maintain a false persona, one that is carefully crafted to elicit admiration, envy, or fear from those around them. It's a game of smoke and mirrors, where perception reigns supreme and reality is but a distant memory.

At its core, the "Law of Fake Image" is fueled by a deep-seated need for validation and acceptance. Individuals like Sumi are driven by an insatiable desire to be seen as successful, desirable, or powerful – regardless of the truth behind their facade. They use social media as their canvas, painting a portrait of a life that exists only in their imagination, while the reality of who they are remains hidden behind closed doors.

But why go to such lengths to maintain a fake image? The answer lies in the power it affords them. By projecting an image of success or superiority, fake individuals are able to manipulate perceptions and wield influence over those around them. They become the envy of their peers, the ones to emulate, the ones to fear – all while hiding the insecurities and vulnerabilities that lie beneath the surface.

Understanding the "Law of Fake Image" is the first step in unmasking the fakers among us. By peeling back the layers of deception and exposing the truth behind their facade, we can reclaim our power to see through the smoke and mirrors and distinguish between authenticity and artifice.

In the next part of this chapter, we'll explore the psychology behind crafting fake personas, especially in the realm of social media. We'll uncover the driving forces behind the need for validation and acceptance, and examine how these forces shape the behaviour of individuals like Sumi. So stay tuned, because the journey into the dark heart of fakery has only just begun.

III. *Spotting the Signs*

It's important to be able to spot deception, particularly when people are projecting a false image of themselves. Individuals who are fake may try to hide behind a glamorous and sophisticated façade, but they often exhibit subtle cues and behaviours that can reveal their true nature. Here are some tell-tale signs to watch out for:

1. Excessive use of social media: Fake individuals are often obsessed with cultivating an online persona. They spend an excessive amount of time on social media, carefully crafting their posts and images to project an image of success and happiness. Be wary of individuals who seem more concerned with their online image than their real-life interactions.

2. Discrepancies between online and offline behaviour: Pay attention to inconsistencies in a person's behaviour between their online persona and their real-life actions. Someone who portrays themselves as confident and outgoing on social media may appear shy or reserved in person, indicating a lack of authenticity.

3. Inconsistencies in stories or claims: Be wary of individuals who constantly change their stories or make exaggerated claims about their achievements or experiences. Fake individuals may embellish the truth in order to impress others and bolster their image of success.

4. Lack of depth or substance: Fake individuals often lack depth or substance in their interactions. They may only focus on superficial topics or engage in shallow conversations, avoiding deeper discussions or meaningful connections.

5. Overemphasis on material possessions: Pay attention to individuals who place an excessive emphasis on material possessions or external markers of success. Fake individuals may use flashy cars, designer clothes, or luxury vacations to bolster their image, but their true worth lies far beyond material wealth.

By keeping these signs in mind, we can become more adept at spotting fake image projections and protecting ourselves from manipulation. In the next part of this chapter, we'll delve deeper into the psychology behind fake image projection by exploring the impact of childhood experiences on personality development and the insatiable need for validation and acceptance. So stay vigilant, because the truth is often hidden in plain sight, waiting to be uncovered by those with the courage to see it.

IV. Peeking Behind the Mask

We have now identified the signs of fake image projection, and it's time to explore the psychology that drives individuals to manipulate their perceptions of reality.

At the core of fake image projection lies a complex web of childhood experiences, insecurities, and the constant need for validation and acceptance. For people like Sumi, the journey into the world of fakery often starts in their early years.

Childhood experiences have a significant role in shaping our personalities and behaviours. For some, childhood is a time of happiness and innocence, filled with love, support, and encouragement. However, for others, it can be a time of trauma, neglect, or emotional turmoil - a time when the seeds of insecurity and self-doubt are planted.

For individuals like Sumi, childhood may have been a battleground, where they were consistently made to feel inadequate or unworthy. Whether it was pressure to excel academically, to conform to societal norms, or to live up to unrealistic expectations, the scars of childhood can leave lasting impressions on the psyche.

These experiences create a void - a sense of emptiness or inadequacy that must be filled at any cost. As a result, people like Sumi turn to fake image projection as a means of coping with their insecurities. They use social media as their stage, crafting elaborate personas that reflect the success, happiness, and validation they so desperately crave.

However, beneath the mask lies a fragile ego, a wounded soul searching for validation in all the wrong places. The need for acceptance drives them to extreme lengths, sacrificing authenticity and integrity in the pursuit of social validation.

Understanding the psychology behind fake image projection is key to identifying the fakers among us. By peeling back the layers of deception and exposing the truth behind their facade, we can regain our ability to distinguish between authenticity and artifice.

In the next part of this chapter, we'll delve deeper into the consequences of fake image projection and explore the damage it can cause to relationships, trust, and self-esteem. So stay tuned, because the journey into the dark heart of fakery has only just begun.

V. Navigating the Maze: Strategies for Spotting Fakes

Now that we've uncovered the twisted psychology behind fake image projection, let's equip ourselves with detailed strategies to navigate this treacherous landscape and emerge unscathed on the other side.

1. **Spotting Fakes with Fierce Precision:**

Train yourself to notice inconsistencies in behaviour, discrepancies between online and offline personas, and signs of superficiality. Listen to your gut feelings when something feels off or too good to be true. Your intuition is a powerful tool for sniffing out fakes. Don't take everything at face value. Verify claims and stories to ensure they align with reality. Look for consistency across different sources of information to validate or debunk claims made by individuals.

1. **Taking Back Control of Our Narrative:**

Establish a clear sense of who you are and what you stand for, so you're less susceptible to external influences. Don't allow others to dictate how you should think, feel, or behave. Assert your autonomy and protect your personal space. Rely on your own internal validation rather than seeking external approval. Trust in your worth and capabilities, regardless of others' opinions. Embrace your true self and express it authentically in all aspects of your life. Authenticity is a powerful antidote to fakery.

By implementing these strategies, we can navigate the maze of fakery with confidence and emerge as champions of authenticity. In the final part of this chapter, we'll reflect on the importance of embracing authenticity in a world that often values illusion over reality. So stay tuned, because the truth is waiting to be uncovered by those with the courage to seek it.

VI. Embracing Reality: The Power of Authenticity

As we approach the end of our exploration into the depths of deception, it is important to reflect on the significance of embracing authenticity in a world that often prioritizes illusion over truth.

Authenticity is much more than just a trendy buzzword. It is a powerful force that influences our relationships, experiences, and sense of self. When we embrace authenticity, we align ourselves with our true values, desires, and aspirations. We become the architects of our own destiny, free from societal expectations and external validation.

However, authenticity is not always easy to achieve. In a world where social media filters and Photoshop dominate, the pressure to conform to unrealistic standards can be overwhelming. We are constantly exposed to images and messages that tell us we are not good enough, smart enough, or successful enough unless we measure up to a certain ideal.

It is time to take back our power and reject the notion that our worth is tied to our online personas or material possessions. It is time to celebrate our imperfections, vulnerabilities, and unique quirks that make us who we are. It is time to embrace the messy, beautiful reality of being human.

So, how can we cultivate authenticity in a world that continually pushes us to be anything but ourselves? It starts with self-awareness – the willingness to look inward and acknowledge the parts of ourselves we may prefer to ignore. It means being honest about our strengths and weaknesses, our triumphs and failures, and our hopes and fears.

But authenticity is not only about being true to ourselves – it is also about showing up authentically in our relationships and interactions with others. It means being open, honest, and genuine in our exchanges, even when it might feel uncomfortable or intimidating. It means building trust through transparency and empathy, and forging deep connections founded on mutual respect and understanding.

In a world where deception and insincerity are commonplace, embracing authenticity is a revolutionary act. It is a declaration of independence from the chains of conformity and a celebration of our unique individuality. It is a reminder that we do not need to be anyone other than ourselves to be worthy of love, respect, and belonging.

So, let us welcome authenticity with open arms and open hearts, and let us inspire others to do the same. Together, we can create a world where authenticity is celebrated, cherished, and revered – a world where the truth shines brightly in the darkness of deception.

And with that, we conclude our journey into the heart of fakery. May we come out of this experience with a newfound sense of clarity, confidence, and authenticity, ready to face the challenges and opportunities that lie ahead?

CHAPTER II

Law of Verbal Domination

"In the orchestra of voices, be wary of the dissonant notes of verbal domination, where confidence conceals a lack of depth, and loudness becomes a mask for insecurity."

I. Introduction

Verbal domination is a subtle yet powerful tactic used by individuals to assert control over conversations, manipulate perceptions, and influence outcomes. It's a phenomenon that often goes unnoticed, lurking beneath the surface of seemingly innocuous interactions. But make no mistake – the impact of verbal domination can be profound, leaving a trail of confusion, resentment, and mistrust in its wake.

Imagine this: you're engaged in a conversation with a friend or colleague, discussing a topic of mutual interest. Everything seems to be going smoothly until you notice a subtle shift in their demeanor. Their tone becomes more assertive, their words more persuasive. Before you know it, they've steered the conversation in a direction that serves their agenda, leaving you feeling unheard and invalidated.

This is the hallmark of verbal domination – the art of controlling conversations through manipulation, intimidation, or coercion. It's a tactic often employed by individuals who seek to assert their dominance, boost their ego, or manipulate others for personal gain. And while the effects of verbal domination may not always be immediately apparent, they can have far-reaching consequences on relationships, self-esteem, and overall well-being.

In my own life, I've encountered individuals who embody the essence of verbal domination. One such person is my college friend, Souman. Souman possesses a keen ability to control conversations and influence others through the power of his words. Whether it's convincing a classmate to adopt his viewpoint or persuading a teacher to see things his way, Souman has mastered the art of verbal manipulation.

I vividly recall an instance where Souman used his verbal prowess to sway a conversation in his favor. We were discussing a classmate's personal struggles with relationships, and Souman seized the opportunity to assert his dominance. With calculated precision, he wove a web of misleading information and out-of-context examples, subtly steering the conversation in a direction that served his agenda. By the end of the conversation, our classmate was convinced by Souman's persuasive arguments, despite the inherent flaws in his logic.

This experience with Souman served as a wake-up call for me – a reminder of the insidious nature of verbal domination and its potential to harm those on the receiving end. It's a phenomenon that demands our attention and vigilance, as we strive to create spaces where open, honest communication can flourish.

In the following sections of this chapter, we'll delve deeper into the intricacies of verbal domination, exploring its underlying motivations, its psychological impact, and its consequences for individuals and relationships. Through personal anecdotes, psychological insights, and practical strategies, we'll equip ourselves with the tools needed to recognize, confront, and overcome verbal domination in our own lives.

So buckle up, because we're about to embark on a journey into the complex world of verbal dynamics, armed with the knowledge and insight to navigate its twists and turns with confidence and clarity.

II. Understanding Verbal Domination

Verbal domination is a multifaceted phenomenon that encompasses a range of behaviours and tactics aimed at controlling conversations and influencing outcomes. At its core, verbal domination is about exerting power and control through language, whether overtly or subtly.

Definition of Verbal Domination:

Verbal domination can be defined as the use of language to assert control, manipulate perceptions, and influence the direction of a conversation. It involves tactics such as interrupting, talking over others, using aggressive language, and employing persuasive techniques to steer discussions in a desired direction.

Examples of Verbal Domination:

Verbal domination can manifest in various ways, both in personal and professional settings. Examples include:

- Interrupting or talking over others to assert dominance in a conversation.

- Using aggressive or condescending language to undermine others' viewpoints.

- Employing persuasive techniques such as guilt-tripping, gaslighting, or manipulation to sway opinions.

- Steering conversations in a direction that serves one's agenda, even if it means disregarding others' perspectives.

- Dominating group discussions by monopolizing speaking time or dismissing opposing viewpoints.

Impact of Verbal Domination:
Verbal domination can have significant consequences for individuals and relationships, including:

- Diminished self-esteem and confidence for those on the receiving end of verbal domination.

- Erosion of trust and respect in relationships, as verbal dominators prioritize their own agenda over the well-being of others.

- Creation of power imbalances in social and professional settings, where those who wield verbal dominance hold disproportionate influence.

- Deterioration of communication dynamics, as open and honest dialogue is stifled by domination tactics.

By understanding the nature of verbal domination and its impact, we can begin to recognize its presence in our own lives and relationships. In the following sections, we'll explore the signs of verbal domination, the underlying psychological motivations behind it, and strategies for effectively confronting and neutralizing its effects.

III. Signs of Verbal Domination

Identifying verbal domination requires a keen eye for subtle and overt behaviours that indicate an attempt to control conversations. Here are some key signs to watch out for:

Changing Behaviour Based on the Presence of Others:
One of the hallmarks of verbal dominators is their ability to shift their behaviour depending on who is around. In private, they may become harsh or dismissive, using a tone that conveys superiority or disdain. However, in the presence of others, they can switch to a more amiable and considerate demeanor, masking their true nature. This chameleon-like behaviour is designed to manipulate how they are perceived by different audiences.

Use of Misleading or Manipulative Language:
Verbal dominators often employ language that is intentionally misleading or manipulative. They might string together unrelated facts or use out-of-context information to build a narrative that serves their purpose. This tactic confuses the listener and makes it difficult to challenge their assertions. For example, Souman's comment to our classmate about "buying a life partner" to solve relationship issues was a misleading way to simplify and control a complex conversation.

Consistently Controlling Conversations:
Those who practice verbal domination are adept at steering conversations in their favor. They often dominate discussions by talking more than others, interrupting frequently, and dismissing or downplaying opposing viewpoints. This constant effort to control the flow of

dialogue ensures that their perspective remains front and center, while others struggle to have their voices heard.

Superficial Listening:

Another common trait is superficial listening. Verbal dominators might pretend to listen, but their primary focus is on planning their next move in the conversation. They often ignore the substance of what others are saying, responding with generic or dismissive comments that steer the conversation back to their agenda.

Recognizing these signs is the first step in protecting ourselves from the manipulative tactics of verbal dominators. In the next section, we will delve into the psychological background that drives individuals to engage in such behaviours, exploring the motivations and experiences that shape their need for verbal control.

IV. Psychological Background

To fully understand verbal domination, it's essential to explore the psychological roots of this behaviour. Verbal domination often stems from deep-seated insecurities, power dynamics, and early life experiences.

Motivations Behind Verbal Domination:

The desire to dominate conversations can be driven by various psychological motivations, including:

Insecurity: Individuals who feel insecure about their own worth or capabilities may use verbal domination as a defense mechanism to assert control and mask their vulnerabilities.

Need for Control: Some people have an intrinsic need to control their environment and the people within it. Verbal domination allows them to maintain a sense of order and predictability.

Ego Gratification: Dominating conversations can be a way for individuals to boost their ego and feel superior to others. It provides a sense of power and validation.

Impact of Childhood Experiences:

Early life experiences play a crucial role in shaping communication styles. Individuals who grew up in environments where they felt unheard or undervalued may develop domineering behaviours as a way to compensate for past neglect. Conversely, those who were overly praised or given excessive power in childhood might develop an inflated sense of entitlement, leading to verbal domination.

Power Dynamics:

Verbal domination is often a reflection of broader power dynamics at play. In social and professional settings, those who hold more power or influence are more likely to engage in dominating behaviours. Understanding these dynamics can help us navigate interactions with verbal dominators more effectively.

By examining the psychological background of verbal domination, we gain insight into why individuals like Souman feel compelled to control conversations. In the next section, we'll discuss the consequences of verbal domination and its impact on relationships, trust, and self-esteem.

V. Personal Experience with Souman

To illustrate the law of verbal domination in action, let me share a personal experience with my friend Souman, who is a master of this tactic. Souman's ability to dominate conversations is both fascinating and troubling, and it offers a clear example of how verbal domination can influence and manipulate.

In our college classroom, there was an incident that perfectly exemplifies Souman's use of verbal domination. One day, he was talking with another classmate about that classmate's personal relationship issues. The classmate was struggling with complex emotions and sought genuine advice and support. Instead of offering empathy and understanding, Souman seized the opportunity to dominate the conversation.

Souman began by subtly shifting the topic to his preferred narrative. He used misleading information and out-of-context examples to steer the discussion. At one point, he advised the classmate to "buy a life partner and live life with her," a comment that was not only inappropriate but completely irrelevant to the classmate's actual situation. Souman's suggestion ignored the nuances of the relationship issues at hand and instead focused on promoting his own simplistic and misguided solution.

What was most striking about this interaction was how Souman's verbal tactics left the classmate convinced and confused. By the end of the conversation, despite the inherent flaws in his logic, Souman had managed to assert his dominance and influence the classmate's perspective. This wasn't an isolated incident; Souman frequently employed similar tactics in different contexts, whether convincing teachers of his point of view or manipulating discussions within our friend group.

Witnessing Souman's behaviour opened my eyes to the insidious nature of verbal domination. It became clear that his actions were not just about winning arguments or being right; they were about controlling the narrative and maintaining power over others. This realization underscored the importance of recognizing and confronting verbal domination to prevent its damaging effects on relationships and communication.

In the next section, we'll explore the broader consequences of verbal domination and how it impacts trust, relationships, and personal growth. Understanding these consequences will further highlight the importance of addressing and mitigating verbal domination in our interactions.

VI. Consequences of Verbal Domination

The consequences of verbal domination extend far beyond individual conversations. This behaviour can have profound and lasting effects on relationships, trust, and personal development. Here are some key consequences to consider:

Damage to Trust and Relationships:
Verbal domination erodes trust and undermines the foundation of healthy relationships. When one person consistently dominates conversations, it creates an imbalance of power and fosters resentment. The dominated party may feel unheard, undervalued, and disrespected, leading to a breakdown in communication and emotional connection.

Undermining of Others' Confidence and Autonomy:
Those who are subjected to verbal domination often experience a decline in self-esteem and confidence. Constantly being overpowered in conversations can make individuals doubt their own opinions and diminish their sense of autonomy. Over time, this can lead to a reluctance to express themselves and a passive approach to communication.

Long-term Effects on Communication Patterns:

Verbal domination can have lasting effects on communication patterns and interpersonal dynamics. Individuals who have been dominated may develop maladaptive communication strategies, such as avoidance or excessive agreeableness, to cope with the dominating behaviour. Conversely, they might adopt domineering tactics themselves as a way to reclaim power in other contexts.

By understanding these consequences, we can better appreciate the importance of addressing verbal domination and promoting healthier communication dynamics. In the following section, we'll discuss practical strategies for dealing with verbal dominators and reclaiming our voice in conversations.

VII. Strategies for Dealing with Verbal Dominators

Confronting verbal domination can be challenging, but it is essential for maintaining healthy communication and asserting your own voice. Here are some strategies to effectively deal with verbal dominators:

Setting Boundaries and Asserting Yourself:

Establish clear boundaries in conversations to prevent being dominated. Politely but firmly assert your right to speak and be heard. For example, you can say, "I would like to finish my point," or "Please let me speak without interruptions." Setting these boundaries helps create a more balanced and respectful dialogue.

Recognizing Manipulative Language and Tactics:

Pay attention to the signs of verbal manipulation, such as the use of unrelated examples, shifting topics, or aggressive language. By recognizing these tactics, you can better navigate the conversation and avoid being swayed by misleading arguments. Question the relevance of their points and ask for clarification when necessary.

Building Confidence and Assertiveness Skills:

Strengthen your communication skills to confidently express your thoughts and opinions. Practice active listening, maintain eye contact, and use assertive body language. Techniques such as the "broken record" method—calmly repeating your point until it is acknowledged—can also be effective in maintaining your stance without escalating the situation.

Using "I" Statements:

When confronting a verbal dominator, use "I" statements to express how their behaviour affects you. For example, "I feel undervalued when I am interrupted," or "I need to finish my thoughts before moving on." This approach focuses on your feelings and needs, making it less likely to provoke defensiveness.

Seeking Support from Others:

If you find it difficult to handle a verbal dominator on your own, seek support from friends, colleagues, or mentors. They can provide additional perspectives, reinforce your boundaries, and help you address the issue collectively. Sometimes, a united front can effectively counteract dominating behaviour.

Evaluating the Relationship:

Assess the overall value and health of your relationship with the verbal dominator. If their behaviour is consistently harmful and resistant to change, it may be necessary to reevaluate the relationship and consider distancing yourself. Prioritize your well-being and surround yourself with individuals who respect and value your voice.

By employing these strategies, you can effectively navigate interactions with verbal dominators and create a more equitable communication dynamic. In the final section of this chapter, we will summarize the key points discussed and emphasize the importance of fostering healthy communication based on mutual respect and empathy.

The concept of verbal domination exposes the manipulative tactics used by individuals to control conversations and assert power. Through personal anecdotes and psychological insights, we have explored the signs, motivations, and consequences of verbal domination. Recognizing verbal domination is essential for maintaining healthy relationships and protecting our sense of self. By setting boundaries, asserting ourselves, and employing effective communication strategies, we can confront and neutralize the effects of verbal domination.

As we move forward, let us aim to cultivate communication dynamics rooted in mutual respect and empathy. Valuing each other's voices and promoting open, honest dialogue can help create a world where verbal domination is replaced by genuine connection and understanding.

CHAPTER III

Law of Alliance

"The Law of Alliance operates through deception, manipulating loyal followers into unwitting pawns."

I. Introduction

In the complex world of deception and manipulation, deceitful people often use the Law of Alliance to consolidate their power and control over others. This tactic involves skillfully building a loyal group of followers who fervently support the deceitful individual without realizing they're being manipulated. Understanding these alliances is crucial for identifying and effectively dealing with deceitful personalities. The Law of Alliance shows how these individuals intricately weave a complex web of influence to stay in control without facing conflicts directly.

This law is very important because it reveals how deceitful individuals exploit social dynamics, turning friends and acquaintances into unwitting pawns. These alliances are not based on genuine respect or mutual support but on manipulation and subjugation. By understanding the Law of Alliance, we can navigate our social environments, identify manipulative behaviours, and shield ourselves from being ensnared in someone else's game of deception.

II. Characteristics of Alliances Formed by Fake Individuals

Formation of a Loyal Group

Fake individuals excel at forming tight-knit groups of followers who, often unknowingly, become their staunch supporters. These alliances are crafted with precision. The fake individual identifies and recruits people who are susceptible to their charm and manipulation. These followers become part of an inner circle, where loyalty to the leader is paramount. The fake person presents themselves as charismatic, knowledgeable, and indispensable, making their followers feel privileged to be part of the group.

Manipulation Tactics

The core of these alliances lies in the manipulation tactics employed by the fake individual. They use flattery, false promises, and selective attention to maintain control over their followers. By providing a sense of belonging and importance, they ensure that their followers remain loyal and obedient. These tactics create a dependency where followers believe that their value and success are tied to the fake individual. The leader carefully crafts their image, using deceit and strategic communication to maintain the illusion of superiority and infallibility.

Blind Loyalty

The loyalty within these groups is often blind. Followers are so captivated by the fake individual's persona that they fail to see the true nature of their leader. They defend and support the leader unconditionally, often ignoring or rationalizing any questionable behaviour. This blind loyalty is reinforced through groupthink, where dissenting opinions are discouraged, and conformity is rewarded. The fake individual thrives in this environment, as it allows them to manipulate and control without facing significant opposition.

III. Group Behaviour in Conflicts

Protecting the Leader

When a conflict arises, the group instinctively rallies to protect their leader. Followers act as the first line of defense, stepping in to shield the fake individual from criticism or confrontation. This protective behaviour is driven by their belief in the leader's infallibility and their desire to maintain the group's cohesion. The fake individual rarely needs to get directly involved in conflicts because their followers handle the defense, perpetuating the leader's image of untouchability.

Attacking Dissenters

If someone within or outside the group challenges the leader, the followers quickly mobilize to attack the dissenter. They use various tactics, such as social ostracism, verbal aggression, and spreading false information, to undermine and discredit the challenger. This collective aggression serves as a deterrent to others who might consider opposing the leader, reinforcing the group's loyalty and the leader's control. The fake individual orchestrates these attacks from the shadows, ensuring their hands remain clean while their followers do the dirty work.

Indirect Control

A key aspect of the Law of Alliance is the fake individual's ability to control the group indirectly. They provide cues and subtle instructions, allowing followers to interpret and act on their behalf. This indirect control makes it difficult to hold the leader accountable, as they can deny direct involvement in any negative actions taken by the group. By maintaining a facade of innocence and detachment, the fake individual preserves their carefully crafted image while continuing to manipulate and dominate through their followers.

IV. Personal Experience with Argha

To provide a real-life example of the Law of Alliance in action, let me share a personal experience with a school friend named Argha. Argha epitomized the manipulative behaviours described above, using his alliance to dominate and control others.

Argha always surrounded himself with a group of loyal followers who viewed him as their supreme leader. These followers, drawn in by his charisma and seemingly confident persona, were eager to defend and support him in all circumstances. They were blind to his true nature, believing that aligning themselves with him was a mark of prestige and power.

One incident during our school days clearly demonstrated Argha's use of the Law of Alliance. A close friend of Argha's, who was considered his right-hand man, got into an argument with Argha over an unclear topic. This argument quickly escalated, and the group members, without understanding the full context, sprang into action to protect their leader. They verbally attacked the dissenting friend, isolating and attempting to break him mentally. Throughout this ordeal, Argha maintained a facade of innocence, pretending not to be involved. However, it was evident to those of us observing from the sidelines that Argha was orchestrating the group's actions.

This incident revealed how Argha manipulated his followers to do his bidding while he remained in the background, controlling the narrative and ensuring his dominance. It was a clear example of how a fake individual leverages the Law of Alliance to maintain power and manipulate others without direct confrontation.

V. Psychological Insights

Need for Validation and Power

The Law of Alliance is deeply rooted in the fake individual's need for validation and power. These individuals often have underlying insecurities and a fear of being exposed. By surrounding themselves with loyal followers, they create an echo chamber that constantly reinforces their desired image. The followers' blind loyalty provides the validation the leader craves, bolstering their self-esteem and sense of control. This need for validation drives their manipulative behaviour, as they seek to maintain the illusion of superiority at all costs.

Impact on Followers

The followers within these alliances are profoundly affected by their involvement. They often lose their sense of individuality and become extensions of the fake leader's will. This dependence on the leader can erode their self-esteem, as their value becomes tied to their loyalty and usefulness to the group. Additionally, followers may adopt manipulative behaviours themselves, mirroring the leader's tactics to gain favor and maintain their position within the alliance. This perpetuates a cycle of manipulation and control, spreading the fake individual's influence further.

Consequences for Dissenters

Those who challenge the fake leader face significant consequences. The collective aggression of the group can be mentally and emotionally devastating for dissenters. They are often ostracized, ridiculed, and attacked, leading to feelings of isolation and self-doubt. The psychological toll of being targeted by the group can be severe, affecting the dissenter's mental health and sense of self-worth. This aggressive response serves as a warning to others, discouraging further challenges to the leader's authority.

VI. Strategies for Dealing with Alliances

Recognizing the Signs

The first step in dealing with alliances formed by fake individuals is to recognize the signs. Pay attention to group dynamics and look for patterns of behaviour where one person seems to wield undue influence. Notice how conflicts are handled within the group—if dissenters are consistently targeted and the leader remains untouched, you might be dealing with a manipulative alliance. Being aware of these signs helps you stay vigilant and avoid falling into the trap of blind loyalty.

Building Your Own Support Network

One of the most effective ways to counteract the influence of a manipulative alliance is to build your own support network. Surround yourself with individuals who value honesty, integrity, and mutual respect. These allies can provide a balanced perspective and emotional support when you face manipulation or attacks. A strong support network can help you stay grounded and confident, making it harder for fake individuals to exert control over you.

Maintaining Independence

Maintaining your independence is crucial when dealing with manipulative alliances. This means staying true to your values and not allowing yourself to be swayed by the group's pressure or the leader's manipulation. Develop a strong sense of self and assert your boundaries clearly. When confronted with manipulation, calmly and confidently express your thoughts and refuse to be drawn into the leader's web of deceit. Independence also involves critical thinking—questioning the leader's motives and actions instead of accepting them at face value.

Confronting the Leader

If you feel confident and safe enough, consider confronting the leader directly. This can be a powerful way to expose their manipulative tactics and disrupt the alliance's dynamics. However, it's important to approach this carefully, as the leader may retaliate. Prepare your arguments, stay calm, and focus on facts rather than emotions. Highlight inconsistencies in their behaviour and how their manipulation affects the group. This can encourage others to see the truth and reconsider their loyalty to the fake leader.

Educating Others

Another strategy is to educate others about the tactics used by fake individuals and the dynamics of manipulative alliances. Share your observations and insights with trusted friends or colleagues, helping them recognize the signs and understand the impact of blind loyalty. By raising awareness, you can empower others to protect themselves and resist manipulation. Education can also foster a culture of critical thinking and mutual respect, reducing the influence of fake individuals in your social or professional circles.

By employing these strategies, you can effectively deal with manipulative alliances and protect yourself from the influence of fake individuals. It's important to remember that while these tactics can be challenging to confront, maintaining your integrity and independence is crucial for your well-being and personal growth.

The Law of Alliance exposes how fake individuals manipulate group dynamics to maintain power and control. Through personal experiences and psychological insights, we've explored the formation of loyal groups, the manipulation tactics used, and the impact on followers and dissenters.

Understanding this law helps us recognize the signs of manipulation and take proactive steps to protect ourselves. By building our support networks, maintaining independence, confronting manipulative leaders, educating others, and seeking professional help when needed, we can navigate these complex social dynamics with confidence and integrity.

As we move forward, let us strive to foster genuine connections and create environments where honesty, respect, and mutual support prevail. In doing so, we can break free from the influence of manipulative alliances and build a more authentic and empowering social landscape.

CHAPTER IV

Law of Superiority

*"Just doing nothing if you think you are
superior, for me you are stupid."*

I. Introduction

Have you ever encountered someone who seems to think they're better than everyone else, even though they're on the same level as you? These people act superior to hide their own insecurities and fakeness. This is the Law of Superiority in action.

People who use the Law of Superiority aim to overpower others and project an image larger than life. In a workplace, social setting, or any group, you might notice individuals who take initiative, which is generally a positive trait. However, some people go beyond simply taking initiative; they act as if they are the only ones capable of leading or managing everything. These individuals are overbearing and controlling, using their supposed superior personality to manipulate and dominate others.

They often pretend to be overly concerned and helpful, but their true motive is control. When others attempt to exhibit the same leadership qualities or initiatives, these fake superiors become offended and insecure. They fear that if someone else can do what they do, they will lose their relevance and power within the group.

Understanding the Law of Superiority is crucial to protect yourself from these manipulative behaviours. By recognizing the signs, you can maintain your independence and prevent being controlled by those who only seek to dominate.

II. *Characteristics of the Law of Superiority*

Overpowering Behaviour

People who use the Law of Superiority often exhibit overpowering behaviour. They act as if they are inherently better than others, even when there is no real difference in status or capability. In conversations and tasks, they dominate, making it difficult for others to contribute or feel valued. This behaviour can be seen in various settings, from classrooms to workplaces, where they impose their will and overshadow others' contributions.

Over-Caring and Controlling Nature

At first glance, these individuals may appear to be caring and helpful. They go out of their way to assist others, offer advice, and take on responsibilities. However, this over-caring demeanor is a tactic to maintain control. By positioning themselves as indispensable, they ensure that others rely on them and view them as leaders. This manipulative approach keeps others dependent and under their influence.

Insecurity and Offense

Despite their outward confidence, individuals using the Law of Superiority are often deeply insecure. They fear losing their status and relevance if others demonstrate similar capabilities. When someone else shows leadership qualities or tries to take initiative, these individuals feel threatened. They may react with offense, becoming defensive or critical to undermine the other person's efforts. This insecurity reveals their true nature and the fragility of their constructed superiority.

Recognizing these characteristics is the first step in identifying and dealing with people who use the Law of Superiority. By understanding their tactics, you can see through their façade and protect yourself from their manipulative influence.

III. Personal Experience with Abhinash

To illustrate the Law of Superiority in action, let me share a personal experience from my college days with a classmate named Abhinash. Abhinash was a master of this law, always trying to dominate and control those around him despite being on the same level as the rest of us.

Abhinash didn't attend class regularly, but whenever he did, he acted like he was the leader of the entire class. He projected an air of superiority, as if the class couldn't function properly without him. This behaviour wasn't limited to academic settings; in any event or group activity, Abhinash acted as though he were more senior and more capable than the rest of us.

One particular incident stands out. I was the class representative at the time, responsible for handling any issues that arose. One day, students from another section got into a fight with some of our classmates. Although I wasn't present at the scene, I quickly learned about the situation from my classmates and decided to take immediate action to resolve the matter.

However, Abhinash, who happened to be present, tried to manipulate me into not taking any action. The reason was clear: the students from the other section involved in the fight were his friends. He wanted to act as the mediator and superior figure, resolving the conflict on his terms. He put in considerable effort to convince me to step aside, portraying himself as the more capable and senior mediator.

This wasn't an isolated incident. Abhinash frequently tried to assert his superiority in various situations, always aiming to control the narrative and the group's dynamics. By being aware of the Law of Superiority, I was able to see through his manipulative tactics and protect myself from his controlling behaviour.

IV. Psychological Insights

Understanding the psychology behind the Law of Superiority can help us better recognize and counteract these behaviours.

Need for Control

At the heart of the Law of Superiority is a deep-seated need for control. Individuals who use this law are often driven by insecurities and fear of being exposed for who they truly are. To compensate, they assert dominance over others, believing that maintaining control will protect them from vulnerability. This need for control manifests in various ways, from dominating conversations to micromanaging tasks and events.

Manipulative Tactics

The tactics employed by those using the Law of Superiority are varied but share a common goal: to maintain the illusion of their superiority. They might offer unsolicited advice, take on responsibilities without delegating, and present themselves as the only capable leader. These actions are designed to make others feel inferior and dependent, reinforcing the manipulator's perceived authority. By keeping others off-balance and uncertain, they strengthen their own position.

Impact on Others

The impact of these manipulative behaviours can be profound. Those who are subjected to the Law of Superiority may feel undermined, devalued, and demoralized. Their contributions are often overlooked, and their confidence can be severely eroded. Over time, this can create a toxic environment where genuine collaboration and mutual respect are stifled. Understanding the psychological motivations behind these tactics can help individuals defend against them and maintain their self-worth.

V. Strategies for Dealing with Superiority

Recognizing the Behaviour

The first step in dealing with individuals who use the Law of Superiority is to recognize the behaviour. Pay attention to patterns of dominance, manipulation, and control. Notice how these individuals react when others try to take initiative or demonstrate leadership qualities. By being aware of these signs, you can better prepare yourself to counteract their tactics.

Maintaining Independence

Maintaining your independence is crucial when dealing with manipulative individuals. This means staying true to your values, making your own decisions, and not allowing yourself to be swayed by their influence. Assert your boundaries clearly and confidently, and don't be afraid to stand up for yourself. By demonstrating that you are not easily controlled, you undermine their attempts to dominate you.

Building Support

Creating a network of allies can help counteract the influence of individuals using the Law of Superiority. Surround yourself with people who value honesty, integrity, and mutual respect. These allies can provide a balanced perspective and support when you face manipulation. Together, you can create a more positive and collaborative environment that resists the toxic influence of fake superiors.

Confronting the Behaviour

If you feel confident and safe enough, consider confronting the superior individual directly. This can be a powerful way to expose their manipulative tactics and disrupt their control. Approach the conversation calmly and focus on specific behaviours rather than personal attacks. Highlight how their actions affect the group and propose more collaborative and respectful ways of interacting. This can encourage others to see through the façade and reconsider their loyalty to the fake superior.

The Law of Superiority reveals how some individuals use manipulation and control to project an image of dominance and hide their insecurities. Through personal experiences and psychological insights, we've explored the characteristics and impact of this behaviour.

By recognizing the signs of superiority, maintaining independence, building supportive networks, and confronting manipulative behaviours, we can protect ourselves and foster healthier, more authentic relationships. Understanding and counteracting the Law of Superiority is essential for creating environments where mutual respect and genuine leadership can thrive.

CHAPTER V

Law of Innocence

"The Law of Innocence is a clever tactic used by manipulators to exploit empathy and kindness, deceiving and emotionally draining others in the process."

I. Introduction

Have you ever met someone who acts very childish despite their age? These people use the Law of Innocence to manipulate others by appearing innocent and helpless. The Law of Innocence states that a person's innocent and childish behaviour is a tactic to make others feel superior and thus easier to manipulate. People naturally tend to protect and help those who seem innocent, which makes them susceptible to this manipulation.

People who use the Law of Innocence speak softly and act like they need constant guidance and support. They craft an image of helplessness, making others feel compelled to assist them. This behaviour is strategic. They want others to believe that they are incapable of handling things on their own, thereby making people around them more willing to help and less likely to challenge them.

Innocence manipulators are particularly adept at creating emotional bonds. They play on human kindness and emotional responses to get what they want. They might present themselves as being in difficult situations, eliciting sympathy and assistance from others. This makes them particularly dangerous, as it can be challenging to identify their true intentions. They can easily turn a person's goodwill against them, making others feel guilty or heartless if they refuse to help.

Let me share a personal experience to illustrate how this law operates in real life. I knew someone who used the Law of Innocence masterfully—her name was Bristi.

II. *Characteristics of the Law of Innocence*

To better understand the Law of Innocence, let's break down its key characteristics:

Childish Behaviour

Individuals who use this law often exhibit childish behaviour. They speak softly, act unsure of themselves, and seem perpetually in need of guidance. This behaviour makes them appear harmless and endearing, which lowers the guard of those around them. Their childlike demeanor evokes a protective response, leading people to overlook their manipulative tendencies.

Pleasing and Praising Others

To further ingratiate themselves, these individuals constantly please and praise others. They shower people with compliments, agree readily, and go out of their way to make others feel special. This creates a sense of loyalty and obligation. People feel flattered and validated, making them more likely to support the manipulator. This tactic ensures that the manipulator is surrounded by individuals who are willing to help and defend them.

Emotional Manipulation

Emotional manipulation is at the core of the Law of Innocence. These individuals frequently present themselves as being in distress or in need of assistance. They share sob stories, exaggerate difficulties, and highlight their supposed vulnerabilities. By playing the victim, they elicit sympathy and compel others to come to their aid. This emotional bond makes it difficult for people to see through the façade.

Playing the Victim

One of the most powerful tools in their arsenal is playing the victim. They depict themselves as being unfairly treated, misunderstood, or oppressed. This tactic diverts attention from their manipulative behaviour and makes others feel guilty for questioning or confronting them. By positioning themselves as victims, they disarm potential critics and secure their manipulative hold over others.

III. Psychological Insights

Human Tendency to Protect the Innocent

One of the primary reasons the Law of Innocence is so effective is due to the human tendency to protect those who seem innocent and vulnerable. From a young age, we are conditioned to care for and shield those who appear weak or helpless. This instinctual response makes it easy for manipulators to exploit our kindness and sense of duty.

Emotional Attachment and Manipulation

Emotional attachment plays a significant role in manipulation. When someone evokes strong emotions, whether through sharing personal struggles or expressing gratitude, it creates a bond. This bond can be leveraged to manipulate others into taking actions they might not otherwise consider. The more emotionally invested someone is, the harder it is for them to see through the manipulation and resist it.

The Danger of Misidentification

One of the dangers of the Law of Innocence is the difficulty in identifying genuine innocence from manipulative behaviour. Genuine innocence and vulnerability are often indistinguishable from the manipulative tactics used by these individuals. This makes it challenging to protect oneself without becoming overly cynical or distrusting. Learning to discern the subtle differences and patterns of behaviour is crucial in safeguarding oneself from such manipulation.

IV. Personal Experience with Bristi

Let me illustrate the Law of Innocence with a personal experience involving Bristi, who adeptly used this tactic to manipulate those around her.

Bristi was a friend of mine whom I initially admired for her seemingly innocent and playful nature. She often spoke softly and used endearing gestures that made her appear harmless and charming. Over time, however, I began to notice a pattern in her behaviour.

One day, Bristi approached me with a seemingly urgent request for help. She claimed that she was struggling with a personal project and needed my expertise to complete it. Despite the task being relatively minor, she portrayed it as overwhelming and beyond her capabilities. Her demeanour suggested vulnerability and helplessness, invoking a strong urge in me to assist her.

After I agreed to help, I noticed a shift in her behaviour. She began to expect my assistance regularly, treating me more like a personal assistant than a friend. Tasks that were initially small favors turned into ongoing responsibilities that she conveniently delegated to me. It became evident that her innocent façade was a strategic ploy to exploit my willingness to help.

Moreover, I later learned from mutual acquaintances that Bristi employed similar tactics with others. She would exaggerate her difficulties or portray herself as a victim in various situations to elicit sympathy and support. Those who refused her requests often faced guilt-tripping or emotional manipulation, making it challenging for them to assert boundaries.

Through this experience, I realized the insidious nature of the Law of Innocence. It preys on our innate desire to protect and assist those who appear vulnerable, ultimately leading to exploitation and manipulation. Bristi's mastery of this law allowed her to manipulate others effortlessly, leaving them feeling used and manipulated.

V. Strategies for Dealing with Innocence Manipulation

Understanding how to navigate interactions with individuals who employ the Law of Innocence is crucial for protecting oneself from manipulation. Here are some effective strategies:

Recognizing the Behaviour

The first step in dealing with innocence manipulation is to recognize the behaviour. Be attentive to signs of exaggerated helplessness, frequent displays of vulnerability, and a pattern of seeking assistance for minor tasks. Manipulators using the Law of Innocence often portray themselves as incapable or in need of constant support, even when the situation does not warrant it.

Maintaining Boundaries

Establishing and maintaining clear boundaries is essential when dealing with manipulative individuals.

Recognize that it is okay to say no and prioritize your own needs and responsibilities. Avoid getting drawn into a caretaker role or feeling obligated to assist someone solely based on their portrayal of innocence. Assert your boundaries firmly and consistently to prevent exploitation.

Building Emotional Resilience

Developing emotional resilience helps in resisting manipulation tactics that target empathy and sympathy. Be mindful of your emotional responses and consider the possibility of manipulation when someone shares personal hardships or portrays themselves as a victim. Maintain a balanced perspective and avoid making decisions solely based on emotional appeals.

Confronting the Manipulator

If you feel comfortable and safe to do so, consider confronting the manipulator directly about their behaviour. Use specific examples to illustrate how their actions have affected you or others. Express your boundaries clearly and assertively, emphasizing the importance of mutual respect in relationships. This approach can disrupt the manipulative cycle and encourage more honest and authentic interactions.

By implementing these strategies, you can mitigate the impact of innocence manipulation and protect yourself from being exploited. Remember that genuine kindness and compassion should be reciprocated in healthy relationships, and it is essential to discern between sincere vulnerability and manipulative tactics.

The Law of Innocence reveals how individuals use a façade of helplessness and vulnerability to manipulate others for personal gain. Through personal experiences and strategic insights, we have explored the characteristics of this manipulation tactic and provided practical strategies for safeguarding oneself.

By recognizing the signs of innocence manipulation, maintaining boundaries, building emotional resilience, and confronting manipulative behaviour when necessary, individuals can empower themselves to navigate relationships more effectively. Understanding and countering the Law of Innocence is essential for fostering genuine connections based on mutual respect and trust.

CHAPTER VI

Law of Over-Friendliness

"Beware of those who smile too widely and offer friendship too quickly; their warmth may be a facade, concealing a heart cold with ulterior motives. "

I. Introduction

Friendship is a cornerstone of human life. True friends stand by us in our most challenging times, offering support and companionship that helps us navigate life's complexities. However, not everyone who presents themselves as a friend has pure intentions. Some individuals use over-friendliness as a tactic to manipulate and control others for their gain.

The Law of Over-Friendliness describes a behaviour where individuals become excessively friendly too quickly, creating an illusion of deep connection and trust. This tactic is often employed to exploit the goodwill of others, using the guise of friendship to achieve selfish objectives. These people seem to be overly interested in your life, eager to help, and quick to establish a sense of camaraderie. But behind this facade lies a calculated strategy to manipulate and take advantage of your trust and resources.

In this chapter, we will explore the characteristics of over-friendliness, delve into the psychological motivations behind it, and share personal experiences to illustrate how this behaviour manifests in real life. By understanding the Law of Over-Friendliness, you can better protect yourself from those who seek to exploit your kindness and trust.

II. Characteristics of Over-Friendliness

Over-friendliness can be disarming and deceptive, making it challenging to discern genuine intentions from manipulative tactics. Here are some key characteristics of over-friendliness to watch out for:

Excessive Friendliness from the Start

Individuals who use the Law of Over-Friendliness often exhibit an unusual level of warmth and enthusiasm from the very beginning. They may act as if they've known you for years, showering you with compliments and making grand gestures of friendship. This sudden rush of friendliness can feel flattering but often serves as a red flag.

Unwarranted and Quick Attempts to Build Deep Connections

These individuals are quick to share personal stories, secrets, and vulnerabilities to create an illusion of intimacy. They may also encourage you to share your own personal information prematurely, building a false sense of trust and closeness. This rapid bonding can feel genuine but is often a strategic move to lower your guard.

Manipulative Motives Behind the Facade of Friendship

Over-friendliness is often a mask for underlying manipulative motives. These individuals might seek to gain your trust to exploit you financially, socially, or emotionally. They use their charm and friendliness to make you feel obligated to help them, support them, or give them access to resources and opportunities they otherwise wouldn't have.

III. Psychological Insights

The Law of Over-Friendliness preys on fundamental aspects of human psychology. Understanding these psychological principles can help us recognize and resist manipulation.

Human Nature's Inclination to Trust Friendly Faces

As social beings, humans are wired to seek connections and trust those who show kindness and warmth. Friendliness often signals safety and camaraderie, which is why we are naturally inclined to trust friendly individuals. Manipulators exploit this inclination, knowing that friendliness can open doors and break down defenses quickly.

Exploitation of Social Bonds for Personal Gain

People who use the Law of Over-Friendliness are adept at forming superficial social bonds that they can leverage for personal gain. These bonds may not be based on genuine care or mutual respect but rather on calculated moves to gain favor, access, or resources. The manipulator's goal is often self-serving, whether it's financial gain, social standing, or emotional support.

Emotional Manipulation Involved in Over-Friendliness

Over-friendly individuals often use emotional manipulation to deepen their control. They may feign vulnerability to elicit sympathy or create scenarios where you feel an obligation to help or support them. By making you feel needed or appreciated, they hook you into their web of manipulation. This emotional entanglement can be hard to break free from, as it plays on our desire to be good friends and supportive individuals.

Recognizing these psychological tactics is the first step in protecting yourself from over-friendliness. It's essential to maintain a healthy scepticism and take the time to truly understand someone's intentions before fully trusting them.

IV. *Personal Experience with Raghab*

As I delve into the intricacies of the Law of Over-Friendliness, let me share a personal experience that perfectly exemplifies how this law operates and the damage it can cause.

In my college classroom, there was a classmate named Raghab. From the very first day, Raghab and I had little interaction, and he seemed just another face in the crowd. However, as the days passed, Raghab began to show an unusual interest in becoming part of my friend circle. He was always around, trying to integrate himself into our group with relentless dedication.

At first, my friends and I were cautious and tried to keep our distance, sensing something off about his eagerness. But Raghab's persistent friendliness and seemingly genuine desire to be our friend wore us down. Eventually, we accepted him into our group, believing his over-friendliness to be harmless.

Weeks turned into months, and Raghab became a familiar presence. He attended group gatherings, participated in discussions, and gradually earned our trust. Everything seemed fine until one day, during the second semester, Raghab called me out of the blue. He sounded distressed and explained that he was in urgent need of financial help. He asked if I could lend him 2000 rupees, promising to return the money within a month.

Despite some initial hesitation, I decided to help him out. I considered him a friend, after all, and believed his story. I transferred the money to him, trusting that he would keep his word. But that's when things took a turn.

As the promised month passed, there was no sign of repayment. Raghab became increasingly elusive, avoiding my calls and making excuses whenever we did manage to speak. He started attending classes irregularly, and when I confronted him about the money, he assured me he would return it soon. However, "soon" never came.

It has been nearly a year and a half, and I have yet to see that money again. Raghab has disappeared from our friend circle and avoids me whenever our paths cross on campus. This experience taught me a valuable lesson about the dangers of over-friendliness. Raghab's charm and persistent friendliness were merely tools he used to manipulate and exploit me for his gain.

Through this ordeal, I realized that trust should be earned gradually and not given freely to those who push their way into our lives with excessive friendliness. Raghab's betrayal was a harsh reminder that not everyone who appears friendly has good intentions. His actions revealed the true nature of his over-friendliness, turning what seemed like a genuine friendship into a painful lesson in manipulation and deceit.

V. Strategies for Dealing with Over-Friendliness

Understanding the Law of Over-Friendliness and recognizing its signs are crucial, but knowing how to effectively deal with such individuals is equally important.

Here are some strategies to protect yourself from manipulative over-friendliness:

Maintain Healthy Skepticism

While it's natural to be friendly and open to new connections, maintaining a degree of skepticism can protect you from being exploited. Don't immediately trust those who try to form a deep bond too quickly. Take your time to get to know people and observe their behaviour over a period before letting them into your inner circle.

Set Boundaries

Establishing clear boundaries is vital in any relationship, especially with those who exhibit over-friendliness. Be firm about your limits and don't be afraid to say no. If someone is pushing too hard to get close or asking for favors too soon, it's a red flag. Setting boundaries will help you maintain control and prevent manipulation.

Trust Your Instincts

Your gut feeling is a powerful tool. If something feels off about a person's over-friendliness, trust your instincts. Don't ignore the subtle cues and warnings your subconscious picks up on. Your instincts can help you detect insincerity and protect you from potential harm.

Observe Their Interactions with Others

Pay attention to how the person interacts with others, not just you. If they exhibit the same level of over-friendliness with everyone, it might indicate a pattern of behaviour used to manipulate multiple people. Watching their interactions can provide valuable insights into their true nature.

Test Their Loyalty and Consistency

True friends are consistent and loyal over time. Test the sincerity of overly friendly individuals by observing their actions in various situations. Are they there for you when you need them, or do they disappear when you require support? Consistency is a key indicator of genuine friendship.

Communicate Openly

If you suspect someone is using over-friendliness to manipulate you, address the issue directly. Open communication can sometimes disarm manipulators, as they often rely on deception and subtlety. By confronting the behaviour, you may discourage further attempts at manipulation.

Seek Advice from Trusted Friends

When in doubt, seek advice from trusted friends or family members. They can provide an outside perspective and may notice things you've overlooked. Their insights can help you make informed decisions about whom to trust and whom to keep at a distance.

In the end, it's about cultivating healthy relationships based on mutual respect, honesty, and genuine care. By being vigilant and discerning, we can protect ourselves from those who seek to manipulate us through over-friendliness and maintain the integrity of our personal and professional lives.

CHAPTER VII

Law of Rumours

*"Rumours are like silent poison, destroying trust
and reputations with a single whispered lie."*

I. Introduction

In the intricate game of manipulation and control, there is a particularly insidious tactic often employed by those with fake personalities: the Law of Rumours. These individuals thrive on spreading false information, creating confusion, and manipulating others through the power of rumours. They are experts at planting seeds of doubt and misinformation, watching as these rumours grow and spread like wildfire, distorting reality and masking their own true intentions.

The Law of Rumours is not just about telling lies; it's about crafting a narrative that serves the manipulator's agenda. Fake people use this tactic to distract, divide, and dominate. By spreading rumours, they create an environment of uncertainty and mistrust, making it difficult for others to see through their façade. The power of a rumour lies in its ability to infiltrate the minds of many, influencing thoughts and behaviours without any concrete evidence.

Imagine being surrounded by whispers, each one designed to make you question your own reality and the intentions of those around you. This is the world that fake people create with their rumours—a world where they can control the narrative and, consequently, the people within it. It is crucial to identify and understand this tactic to protect oneself from its damaging effects.

In this chapter, we will delve into the nature of rumours, explore how they are spread, and discuss the psychological impact they have on individuals and groups. Through personal anecdotes and practical advice, we aim to equip you with the knowledge and tools necessary to recognize and combat the Law of Rumours.

II. *The Nature of Rumours*

Rumours are a potent tool in the arsenal of manipulators. They thrive on ambiguity, spreading half-truths and outright lies to create a smokescreen around their true intentions. At their core, rumours are pieces of information that lack verification but are widely disseminated, often gaining traction due to their provocative or scandalous nature. The human mind is naturally curious and drawn to novelty, which makes rumours particularly effective.

The psychology behind why people believe and spread rumours is multifaceted. First, there's a social aspect. People often share rumours to bond with others, creating a sense of shared knowledge and exclusivity. Being the bearer of a rumour can make someone feel important and included in a group. Additionally, rumours often play on existing fears and prejudices, making them more believable. When a rumour confirms a person's existing beliefs or suspicions, they are more likely to accept it as true.

Rumours can have devastating impacts on individuals and groups. They can tarnish reputations, destroy relationships, and create an atmosphere of distrust and hostility. Once a rumour takes hold, it can be incredibly difficult to disprove, as the mere act of defending against it can reinforce its perceived legitimacy. The damage done by a rumour can linger long after the truth is revealed, leaving scars that are not easily healed.

In a social or professional setting, the spread of rumours can lead to a toxic environment. People may become suspicious of each other, alliances can form based on misinformation, and the overall morale can plummet. The manipulator, meanwhile, sits back and watches as their handiwork creates chaos, using the confusion to their advantage.

Understanding the nature of rumours is the first step in combating them. By recognizing the signs of rumour-mongering and understanding the motivations behind it, we can better protect ourselves and our communities from its harmful effects.

III. Identifying the Spreaders of Rumours

To effectively counteract the Law of Rumours, it's crucial to identify the individuals who frequently spread them. These rumour-mongers often exhibit specific characteristics and behaviours that can serve as warning signs.

Inconsistent Behaviour: Rumour spreaders often show inconsistencies in their behaviour and stories. They might tell different versions of the same event to different people, adjusting the narrative to suit their audience and sow confusion.

Attention-Seeking: These individuals crave attention and often use rumours to place themselves at the center of social interactions. They thrive on the drama and conflict that rumours generate, enjoying the power and influence they gain in the process.

Gossip Habit: A chronic rumour spreader usually has a habit of gossiping about others. They seem to always have some "juicy" information to share, often painting themselves as being "in the know" or having exclusive access to insider information.

Manipulative Tendencies: They are skilled manipulators who use rumours as a tool to achieve their goals. Whether it's gaining favor, undermining rivals, or diverting attention from their own shortcomings, their use of rumours is deliberate and strategic.

Lack of Accountability: When confronted about spreading false information, these individuals rarely take responsibility. Instead, they deflect blame, often claiming they "heard it from someone else" or that they were just "passing on what they were told."

Observant and Opportunistic: Rumour spreaders are keen observers of social dynamics. They know who to target and when to strike, capitalizing on moments of vulnerability or tension to introduce their rumours and watch them take root.

By being aware of these signs, you can better protect yourself from the harmful effects of rumours. When you encounter someone exhibiting these behaviours, it's essential to approach their information with skepticism and verify facts independently whenever possible.

IV. My Real-Life Experience with Rumours

Let me share a personal experience that highlights the destructive power of the Law of Rumours. There was a person I knew, Sana, who mastered this law to manipulate and control her environment. She was adept at spreading rumours, using them to create discord and assert her dominance.

When I was the class representative in college, Sana used the Law of Rumours against me. There was a teacher known for his strict adherence to rules. Sana disliked him because of his strict behaviour. As the class representative, I followed the teacher's guidelines closely, which led Sana to believe that the teacher was favouring me during exams and internal evaluations.

To undermine my position and create chaos, Sana spread a rumour around the class, claiming that I was receiving extra marks because the teacher favoured me. This rumour spread like wildfire, fuelled by Sana's manipulative skills and the existing tensions within the class. Many students believed her, and the classroom atmosphere became hostile and divided.

Despite my efforts to communicate the truth and clear my name, the damage was done. The rumour had taken root, and many classmates viewed me with suspicion and resentment. Sana's rumour had successfully manipulated the class's perception, isolating me and creating a toxic environment.

This experience taught me the importance of recognizing and addressing rumours quickly. It also highlighted how easily people can be swayed by misinformation and the destructive impact it can have on personal and communal relationships.

V. Strategies to Combat Rumours

Understanding how to combat the Law of Rumours is essential for maintaining a healthy and honest environment. Here are some strategies to protect yourself and others from the damage caused by rumours:

Verify Information: Always verify the information before accepting it as true. Check the sources and seek out multiple perspectives to get a complete and accurate picture. Don't rely on hearsay; instead, look for concrete evidence.

Address Rumours Directly: If you become aware of a rumour, address it head-on. Confront the person spreading the rumour and ask for clarification. Sometimes, bringing the rumour into the open can diminish its power.

Promote Transparency: Encourage transparency in your social and professional circles. Open communication and honesty can reduce the impact of rumours, as people are less likely to believe false information when they have access to the truth.

Educate Others: Help others understand the harmful effects of rumours. Share your knowledge about the tactics used by rumour-mongers and encourage critical thinking. When people are aware of the manipulative nature of rumours, they are less likely to be influenced by them.

Build a Positive Reputation: Maintain a positive reputation through consistent, honest behaviour. When people know you as someone who is trustworthy and reliable, they are less likely to believe negative rumours about you.

Support Victims of Rumours: Offer support to those who are targeted by rumours. Stand by them and help them clear their name. Collective support can help counteract the isolation and damage caused by rumours.

Create a Code of Conduct: In professional settings, establish a code of conduct that discourages gossip and rumour-mongering. Encourage a culture of respect and integrity, where people feel safe and valued.

Be Cautious with Personal Information: Be mindful of the personal information you share with others. Avoid oversharing, especially with individuals who have a tendency to spread rumours.

By implementing these strategies, you can reduce the impact of rumours and create an environment where truth and integrity are valued over deceit and manipulation.

The Law of Rumours is a potent tool used by manipulators to create chaos and control their environment. However, by understanding the nature of rumours and recognizing the behaviours of those who spread them, we can protect ourselves and our communities.

Awareness and proactive action are key to combating rumours. By verifying information, addressing rumours directly, promoting transparency, and supporting victims, we can create a culture of integrity and trust. It's essential to stay vigilant and not be swayed by misinformation, ensuring that we uphold the values of honesty and respect.

Remember, the power of rumours lies in their ability to spread unchecked. By taking a stand against them and fostering an environment of open communication and truth, we can diminish their impact and build a stronger, more cohesive community.

CHAPTER VIII

Law of People Pleasing

"People pleasing is the art of wearing a mask so convincingly that even you start to believe it. Beware, for in flattering others, you may lose yourself."

I. Introduction

In the intricate dance of social interactions, the Law of People Pleasing is a powerful yet deceptive tactic employed by individuals who seek to manipulate and control those around them. People pleasing, on the surface, may appear as harmless charm or benign agreeability. However, beneath this façade often lies a carefully crafted strategy designed to bend others to their will.

People pleasers are masters of superficial friendliness. They will shower you with compliments, agree with everything you say, and seem to support your every idea. At first glance, this might seem like genuine camaraderie. However, this behaviour is rarely as innocent as it appears. The underlying truth is that people pleasers have motives that go beyond mere kindness—they use their charm and agreeability as tools of manipulation.

Their approach is calculated. They understand that by appearing to be supportive and agreeable, they can gain trust and influence. But the reality is that their actions are driven by self-interest. The discrepancy between their outward behaviour and their true intentions can be startling. While they might seem like the ultimate allies or friends, their real goal is often to gain control, extract favors, or manipulate situations to their advantage.

In social settings, this manipulation can be subtle. People pleasers avoid confrontation and conflict, presenting themselves as easygoing and accommodating. They will say what they think others want to hear, often to the detriment of honesty and authenticity. This makes them dangerous, as their true motives are hidden behind a veneer of charm and agreeable behaviour.

Recognizing the Law of People Pleasing is crucial for navigating relationships and interactions. By understanding the tactics employed by these individuals, you can better protect yourself from their manipulation and maintain genuine, trustworthy relationships. In the chapters ahead, we will delve deeper into the characteristics of people pleasers, uncover their hidden motives, and explore strategies for handling such individuals effectively.

II. Characteristics of a People Pleaser

Understanding the Law of People Pleasing requires recognizing the key traits that define a people pleaser. These individuals exhibit specific behaviours that set them apart from genuinely kind and supportive people. Here's a closer look at these characteristics:

Persistent Flattery and Compliments:

People pleasers are often seen showering others with excessive praise. They seem to have a never-ending supply of compliments, making you feel valued and admired. While this might initially seem like a sign of genuine affection, it is often a tactic to win favor and lower your defenses. Their flattery is not always heartfelt but strategically designed to manipulate.

Agreeability to Everything:

One of the most telling signs of a people pleaser is their unwavering agreement with whatever you say. They will nod along, affirm your opinions, and express enthusiasm for your ideas, even if they don't genuinely agree. This constant affirmation is not necessarily a sign of support but rather a means to ingratiate themselves and maintain influence over you.

Avoidance of Conflict and Confrontation:

People pleasers go to great lengths to avoid disagreements. They will sidestep difficult conversations and suppress their own opinions to keep the peace. Their aversion to conflict can make them seem easy to get along with, but it also means they are not always honest or straightforward. This avoidance can prevent meaningful dialogue and lead to unresolved issues.

Discrepancy Between Words and Actions:

While people pleasers may speak in supportive and agreeable terms, their actions often tell a different story. They may verbally support your ideas but fail to back them up with concrete actions. This discrepancy is a red flag that their outward behaviour is not a true reflection of their intentions.

Creating a False Sense of Intimacy:

People pleasers often try to create a sense of closeness quickly. They may share personal details, engage in overly familiar behaviour, or act as though they've known you forever. This false intimacy is designed to lower your guard and make you more susceptible to their manipulation.

Overly Accommodating Behaviour:

They will go out of their way to be accommodating, often to the point of self-sacrifice. This can involve taking on extra work, making significant compromises, or doing favors that seem generous but are often done with the expectation of something in return.

Recognizing these traits can help you identify people pleasers in your life. While their behaviour may initially seem friendly and supportive, it's important to remain vigilant and assess their true motives. In the next sections, we will explore the hidden motives behind people pleasing, strategies to handle these individuals, and how to protect yourself from their manipulation.

III. The Hidden Motives Behind People Pleasing

At first glance, people pleasers might seem like genuinely nice individuals who just want to get along with everyone. However, their outwardly pleasant demeanor often masks deeper, self-serving motives. Here's a closer look at the hidden agendas that drive people pleasers:

Manipulation for Personal Gain:

The primary motive behind people pleasing is often personal gain. By being excessively agreeable and flattering, people pleasers aim to build a network of supporters who are more likely to do favors for them or support their ambitions. They leverage their charm to create a favorable environment where they can achieve their own goals, often at the expense of others.

Building a Facade of Friendliness:

People pleasers use their friendly behaviour to construct a facade of trustworthiness and likability. This facade can make them appear indispensable or irreplaceable. The goal is to create a perception of themselves as helpful and supportive, which can make it easier for them to manipulate others into complying with their wishes.

Masking True Intentions:

The sweetness and agreeability of people pleasers are often a mask for their true intentions. They may agree with you on the surface while secretly undermining your plans or competing with you. Their outward behaviour is designed to conceal their real motives, whether it's gaining control, securing advantages, or manipulating situations to their benefit.

Gaining Control Through Dependency:

By ingratiating themselves with others, people pleasers create a sense of dependency. When you rely on their supposed support, you may become more susceptible to their influence. They cultivate relationships where they appear as the sole provider of help or guidance, making it difficult for others to challenge or question their actions.

Avoiding Responsibility:

People pleasers often use their agreeable nature to avoid taking responsibility. They may agree to help or support others but then find excuses to avoid fulfilling their commitments. This behaviour allows them to maintain their favorable image while sidestepping the accountability of actually delivering on their promises.

Exploiting Emotional Sensitivity:

People pleasers are adept at exploiting the emotional sensitivity of others. They use flattery and charm to evoke positive feelings and create a bond that makes it harder for others to confront them about their true motives. This emotional manipulation is a key tactic in ensuring that their ulterior motives remain concealed.

IV. Strategies for Managing Interactions with People Pleasers

Navigating relationships with people pleasers requires a strategic approach. Since their intentions are often hidden behind a veneer of friendliness, it's important to handle these interactions with care and awareness. Here's how you can effectively manage relationships with people pleasers:

Set Clear Boundaries:

Establishing clear and firm boundaries is crucial when dealing with people pleasers. Clearly define what you are comfortable with and what you are not. Make it known when you are unwilling to participate in their manipulative tactics or when their behaviour becomes intrusive. Enforcing boundaries helps protect you from being taken advantage of and maintains a healthy distance.

Be Cautious with Trust:

People pleasers often work hard to gain your trust, but it's essential to remain cautious. Don't be too quick to share personal information or confide in them until you have had time to observe their true intentions. Trust should be earned through consistent and genuine behaviour, not just through superficial charm and flattery.

Evaluate Their Actions:

Pay close attention to the actions of people pleasers rather than just their words. While they may speak in flattering and agreeable terms, their actions will reveal their true motives. Look for discrepancies between what they say and what they do. If their actions consistently show self-serving behaviour or a lack of follow-through, it's a red flag.

Maintain Your Independence:

People pleasers often seek to make you dependent on them for approval or support. Resist this manipulation by maintaining your independence. Make decisions based on your own judgment and priorities, rather than being swayed by their attempts to please or flatter you. Your autonomy is crucial for avoiding their influence.

Communicate Directly:

When addressing issues with people pleasers, communicate directly and assertively. Avoid being overly accommodating or vague. Clearly express your concerns and expectations without being influenced by their attempts to appease you. Direct communication helps prevent misunderstandings and reinforces your boundaries.

Recognize the Signs of Manipulation:

Be aware of common manipulation tactics used by people pleasers, such as excessive flattery, avoidance of responsibility, and creating a false sense of intimacy. By recognizing these signs, you can better navigate interactions and avoid falling victim to their manipulative strategies.

Limit Interaction if Necessary:

If a people pleaser's behaviour becomes too disruptive or harmful, it may be necessary to limit your interaction with them. Reducing contact can help you regain control and protect your well-being. You don't have to completely sever ties, but minimizing interactions can reduce their influence over you.

V. Personal Impact and Examples

In my own experience, I encountered someone who mastered the Law of People Pleasing. Her name was

Madhu. From the beginning, Madhu went out of her way to be incredibly friendly and supportive. She was always complimenting my work and agreeing with my ideas, making me feel like we had a strong, genuine connection.

However, when it came time for her to ask for a favour, she was quick to present herself as someone in need, creating a sense of obligation. She never fought for herself or stood up for her own opinions. Instead, she used her seemingly endless friendliness to get what she wanted from those around her.

Eventually, I realized that her behaviour was a strategic ploy. The facade of friendship was just that—a facade. By understanding the Law of People Pleasing, I was able to protect myself from her manipulative tactics and avoid becoming another pawn in her game.

The Law of People Pleasing is a powerful tactic used to manipulate and control others through excessive charm and flattery. By recognizing the signs and employing strategies to manage these relationships, you can protect yourself from their influence and maintain healthier interactions. Remember, true friendship and support are built on mutual respect and honesty, not on manipulation and deceit.

CHAPTER IX

Law of Always Correct

"The Law of Always Correct blinds us to the truth by fostering an illusion of infallibility, leaving no room for growth and eroding genuine dialogue."

I. Introduction

Imagine being around someone who, no matter what the situation, insists that they are always right. They're the type who will argue that the sun didn't rise if they say so, or insist that their version of the truth is the only one that matters. This is the essence of the Law of Always Correct. This law is not just about being confident or having a strong opinion. It's about a pervasive need to be seen as infallible, to have every assertion validated as true regardless of the actual facts. People who operate under this law are often unaware of how their behaviour impacts those around them. To them, being right is not just a preference but a fundamental aspect of their identity.

In our daily interactions, encountering someone who embodies the Law of Always Correct can be exhausting. Their insistence on being right can strain relationships and create an environment where disagreement is not just uncomfortable but almost impossible. They manipulate conversations to ensure their viewpoint prevails, often disregarding evidence or logic in favor of their unshakeable belief in their correctness.

Recognizing this behaviour is crucial because it often masks deeper issues—insecurities, a need for control, or a fear of being vulnerable. These individuals may not always be overtly malicious; their behaviour might stem from a subconscious desire to protect their self-image or avoid confronting their own flaws. Understanding and identifying this behaviour helps us navigate interactions with such individuals and protect our own mental well-being. In this chapter, we'll explore the characteristics of people who use the Law of Always Correct, dive into real-life experiences that illustrate this behaviour, and discuss strategies for dealing with them effectively.

II. *Characteristics of the Law of Always Correct*

Infallibility Complex

People who operate under the Law of Always Correct believe they are incapable of being wrong. This belief is not merely about having strong opinions; it's about an unwavering certainty that their perspective is the absolute truth. Such individuals are driven by an intense need to be perceived as perfect and knowledgeable. When faced with conflicting information, they often dismiss it outright rather than reconsidering their stance.

Defensive Tactics

When their assertions are challenged, these individuals employ various tactics to defend their position. They might:

Dismiss Evidence: They ignore or belittle any facts or data that contradict their claims. Instead of addressing the evidence, they might change the topic or claim that the evidence is flawed.

Shift Blame: If they are proven wrong, they quickly deflect responsibility, often by blaming others or external factors. They might say things like, "You misunderstood," or "It's not my fault that things went wrong."

Reframe the Argument: They alter the context of the discussion to suit their narrative, making it difficult for others to counter their points effectively.

Unconscious Nature of the Behaviour

Interestingly, the Law of Always Correct is not always a deliberate manipulation. For many, it is an unconscious defense mechanism. These individuals may genuinely believe in their infallibility, driven by deep-seated fears or insecurities. They might not even realize the extent to which their behaviour affects others or the extent of their own inflexibility.

In the next section, we will delve into a real-life example that illustrates how the Law of Always Correct manifests and the impact it has on relationships. Through personal experience, we will see how this behaviour plays out and the challenges it presents.

III. Real-Life Examples

To illustrate the Law of Always Correct, let me share a personal experience with a relative who epitomizes this behaviour. This individual has a remarkable talent for asserting that their version of events is the only valid one, regardless of the actual circumstances.

One incident stands out vividly. During a family gathering, a discussion arose about the timing of a local event. Everyone had different recollections, but this relative was adamant that their version was the absolute truth. Despite multiple people providing conflicting accounts and evidence to the contrary, they continued to argue with unwavering certainty. They insisted that their memory was flawless and that anyone who disagreed was simply mistaken.

When the conversation heated up and it became clear that they were in the minority, they didn't concede or re-evaluate their stance. Instead, they doubled down, dismissing others' input as irrelevant and even suggesting that the disagreement was due to others' lack of knowledge. Their refusal to admit any possibility of being wrong turned the discussion into a battleground where only their perspective was deemed valid.

This behaviour had several consequences:

Frustration and Alienation: The rest of the family, witnessing this rigid stance, felt frustrated and alienated. Conversations became tense, as it was clear that any differing opinion was not welcomed or considered. This led to a toxic atmosphere where open discussion was stifled, and mutual respect was eroded.

Loss of Credibility: Over time, this relative's insistence on always being right diminished their credibility. Family members began to view their opinions with skepticism, recognizing that their need to be correct often overshadowed the actual facts.

Escalation of Conflict: The constant need to prove themselves right turned minor disagreements into major conflicts. Small misunderstandings became significant disputes, causing unnecessary strife within the family dynamic.

Broader Implications

This experience is not an isolated case. The Law of Always Correct can manifest in various settings, from professional environments to casual social interactions. Individuals who exhibit this behaviour may unintentionally foster an environment of distrust and conflict, making it difficult for others to engage in constructive dialogue.

IV. Psychological Underpinnings

Insecurity and Self-Image

At the core of the Law of Always Correct often lies a deep-seated insecurity. People who adhere to this law may struggle with a fragile self-image or fear of inadequacy. By positioning themselves as always right, they create a façade of competence and confidence that masks their internal struggles. This behaviour serves as a defense mechanism to protect their ego and avoid confronting their own vulnerabilities.

Fear of Vulnerability

Admitting mistakes or acknowledging differing viewpoints requires vulnerability—something that individuals using the Law of Always Correct are often unwilling to tolerate. For them, being wrong is synonymous with failure or weakness. To avoid this, they cling to their assertions with rigid certainty, even in the face of overwhelming evidence to the contrary. This fear of vulnerability drives them to double down on their positions, regardless of how incorrect they may be.

Need for Control

Maintaining the image of being always correct also satisfies a need for control. By dominating conversations and insisting on their correctness, these individuals exert power over the social dynamics around them. They control the narrative and dictate the terms of engagement, which can give them a false sense of security and dominance.

This need for control can stem from a lack of control in other areas of their lives, making the Law of Always Correct a way to exert influence and maintain their perceived superiority.

Cognitive Dissonance

Cognitive dissonance plays a role in this behaviour as well. When confronted with information that contradicts their beliefs, individuals adhering to the Law of Always Correct experience psychological discomfort. To resolve this dissonance, they might dismiss, distort, or ignore the conflicting information rather than reconcile their views with reality. This mental gymnastics allows them to maintain their self-image as always right while avoiding the discomfort of admitting fault.

V. Strategies for Managing Interactions

1. Set Boundaries

When dealing with individuals who consistently use the Law of Always Correct, it's crucial to establish clear boundaries. Limit the scope of discussions where you know their need to be right will dominate. By setting boundaries, you can protect yourself from unnecessary conflict and maintain your mental well-being.

2. Stay Calm and Objective

Engaging with such individuals requires patience and a calm demeanor. Approach discussions with an objective mindset, focusing on facts rather than getting drawn into emotional arguments. By remaining calm, you reduce the chances of escalating the situation and can present your viewpoints more effectively.

3. Avoid Personalizing Their Behaviour

Remember that their need to be always correct is a reflection of their own issues and insecurities, not a personal attack on you. By not taking their behaviour personally, you can better manage your interactions and maintain your own sense of self-worth.

4. Choose Your Battles

Decide when it's worth engaging in debate and when it's better to walk away. Some arguments may not be worth pursuing, especially if the other party is unlikely to reconsider their stance. Prioritize your time and energy on discussions that are productive and meaningful.

The Law of Always Correct is a powerful yet detrimental behaviour that influences personal and professional dynamics. By understanding its psychological underpinnings and implementing effective management strategies, you can navigate interactions with individuals who embody this law and protect your own well-being. Moreover, fostering an environment of respect and openness can help counteract the negative effects and promote more constructive and supportive relationships.

CHAPTER X

Law of Big Words

"Grandiose words are often just a smokescreen for empty promises; beware of those who speak loudly but deliver little."

I. Introduction

Have you ever met someone who constantly boasts about their achievements, skills, or experiences but, in reality, falls short of delivering on those grand claims? This is the essence of the Law of Big Words. It's a tactic used by individuals who inflate their accomplishments and abilities with exaggerated or grandiose statements, but when it comes to proving their worth through actual achievements or actions, they fall significantly short.

People who use the Law of Big Words often rely on their ability to talk a big game to impress or intimidate others. They may use impressive language and make bold promises, creating an illusion of greatness that rarely aligns with their true capabilities. This facade is designed to manipulate perceptions and create an impression of superiority, even though their real-life actions and accomplishments do not reflect the same level of success.

The Law of Big Words can be particularly damaging because it preys on the perceptions and expectations of others. When individuals make lofty claims without the substance to back them up, it can lead others to place undue trust or expectations on them, only to be disappointed later on. Recognizing this behaviour is crucial for avoiding manipulation and protecting oneself from the deceptive tactics of those who rely on empty rhetoric.

In this chapter, we'll delve into the characteristics of the Law of Big Words, explore psychological insights behind it, and provide strategies for identifying and dealing with individuals who use this manipulative tactic. Through a personal experience with someone who exemplified this law, we'll illustrate how to navigate and counteract the empty promises and grandiose claims that can often cloud judgment and lead to disillusionment.

II. Characteristics of the Law of Big Words

1. Grandiose Claims

One of the primary traits of the Law of Big Words is the frequent use of grandiose claims. Individuals who employ this law often boast about their achievements, skills, or future plans in a manner that seems impressive but lacks tangible proof. They might declare themselves as experts in a field they have little experience in or promise future successes that they are unlikely to achieve. Their language is filled with superlatives and exaggerated statements designed to dazzle and impress those around them.

2. Lack of Action

While these individuals are quick to speak about their achievements and future plans, they are notably slow when it comes to taking concrete actions. They prefer to talk rather than do, and their grandiose claims rarely translate into actual results. This lack of action reveals the disparity between their words and their true capabilities. When scrutinized, the gaps between their promises and their actual performance become glaringly obvious.

3. Showmanship Over Substance

People using the Law of Big Words often rely on showmanship to maintain their façade. They might dress in a certain way, use elaborate language, or engage in dramatic storytelling to enhance their image. This focus on presentation rather than substance is a key indicator of their reliance on empty promises. Their impressive demeanor and eloquent speech serve as a smokescreen to divert attention from the lack of real achievements.

4. Exploitation of Insecurities

Another characteristic of the Law of Big Words is the exploitation of others' insecurities. Manipulators often target individuals who are vulnerable or lack confidence, using their grand claims to intimidate or impress. By creating an aura of superiority, they aim to make others feel inadequate or inferior, which can make it easier to manipulate them. This exploitation can lead to others placing undue trust or reliance on these individuals, only to be let down later.

III. Psychological Insights

1. The Appeal of Big Words

The allure of grandiose claims is rooted in human psychology. Big words and impressive promises have a strong emotional appeal. They evoke admiration, respect, or even envy, making it easy for people to be drawn in. This appeal is particularly potent in social settings where status and success are highly valued. Individuals who use the Law of Big Words exploit this appeal to create an image of greatness and authority, capitalizing on the desire of others to associate with perceived success.

2. The Discrepancy Between Words and Actions

A critical psychological insight is the cognitive dissonance that occurs when there's a gap between what people say and what they actually do. This discrepancy can cause confusion and frustration among those who take the claims at face value. Over time, as actions fail to align with promises, the inconsistency becomes more apparent. This recognition of the gap between words and actions can lead to a loss of trust and respect for the individual making the grand claims.

3. Recognizing the Pattern

Understanding the psychological pattern behind the Law of Big Words involves recognizing certain behavioural indicators. Pay attention to the consistency of their claims, the frequency of their promises, and the gap between their verbal boasts and actual results. Individuals who rely on this law often exhibit a pattern of excessive talking about their achievements or future plans without corresponding actions to support those claims. Recognizing this pattern can help in identifying when someone is more interested in creating an illusion than in delivering real outcomes.

4. Psychological Impact on Others

The psychological impact on those who interact with individuals using the Law of Big Words can be profound. People may experience heightened expectations and subsequent disappointment when the reality fails to meet the promises. This can lead to feelings of frustration, inadequacy, or even self-doubt. Being aware of this impact can help individuals manage their expectations and maintain a critical perspective when dealing with those who rely on grandiose claims.

IV. Personal Experience with Aakash

Let me introduce you to Aakash, a master of the Law of Big Words. I met Aakash when I was around 15 or 16 years old, and he was a bit older, in his early 20s. We crossed paths at a relative's house where he made an indelible impression. At that time, I was an introverted teenager, lacking confidence and struggling with self-esteem. Aakash, on the other hand, projected an air of superiority and expertise.

During our meeting, Aakash took it upon himself to demonstrate his supposed superiority. He engaged me in a conversation about English grammar and made it clear that he considered himself an expert in the subject. His manner was patronizing, and he seemed to revel in making me feel inferior. He spoke in grand terms about his achievements, claiming to be a great teacher and suggesting that his insights were invaluable.

Aakash's behaviour was not just limited to verbal boasts. He used his position as an older, more experienced individual to intimidate me, making me feel inadequate. He had a way of weaving his grand claims into the conversation, painting himself as someone who had achieved far more than he actually had. This was his way of asserting dominance and attempting to make me feel small.

In retrospect, Aakash's grandiose claims and showy demeanor were classic examples of the Law of Big Words in action. His approach was designed to dazzle and intimidate rather than to genuinely connect or contribute. He relied on impressive language and self-aggrandizing statements to create an illusion of greatness. His behaviour was a tactic to overshadow others and to project an image of success that was not backed by actual achievements.

Over time, I learned that Aakash's claims were far removed from reality. Despite his boasts about being a great teacher and a successful individual, his life took a different turn. I later discovered that he had become a drug addict, and his grand promises and claims had turned out to be nothing more than hollow words. This shift from boasting to failure highlighted the stark contrast between his words and his reality.

V. Strategies for Dealing with Big Words Manipulation

1. Evaluating Actions vs. Words

The first and most effective strategy in dealing with the Law of Big Words is to closely evaluate the discrepancy between an individual's words and their actions. When someone makes grandiose claims, it's crucial to scrutinize their actual achievements and behaviours. Pay attention to whether their promises are backed by tangible results. If their actions consistently fall short of their claims, it's a clear indicator of their reliance on empty rhetoric.

To assess this, consider:

- **Track Record**: Look at their past achievements and whether they align with their current claims.
- **Consistency**: Observe if their actions consistently reflect the level of success they boast about.
- **Evidence**: Seek concrete evidence of their accomplishments rather than relying on verbal assurances.

2. Maintaining Self-Confidence

When interacting with individuals who use the Law of Big Words, maintaining your own self-confidence is crucial. Such individuals often use their grandiose claims to intimidate or belittle others. By staying confident in your own abilities and achievements, you can better resist their attempts to undermine you. Remember, their need to boast is often a reflection of their own insecurities.

Tips for maintaining confidence:

- **Focus on Your Strengths**: Remind yourself of your own achievements and strengths.
- **Set Boundaries**: Don't let their inflated claims diminish your self-worth or influence your decisions.
- **Seek Support**: Surround yourself with people who value and support you, providing a buffer against manipulative tactics.

3. Setting Realistic Expectations

When dealing with individuals who rely on the Law of Big Words, it's important to set realistic expectations and not be swayed by their grand promises. Understand that their claims are often designed to impress rather than to deliver. By setting practical and achievable expectations, you can protect yourself from disappointment and manage interactions more effectively.

Steps to set realistic expectations:

- **Clarify Goals**: Define what you expect from the relationship or interaction based on realistic outcomes.
- **Monitor Progress**: Regularly check if the promises are being fulfilled or if the individual is falling short.
- **Be Prepared**: Be ready for potential letdowns if their claims do not match their actual performance.

4. Avoiding Emotional Reactions

Emotional reactions can cloud judgment and make it harder to see through manipulative tactics. Individuals who use the Law of Big Words may attempt to provoke emotional responses to gain an advantage. Staying calm and rational helps in assessing the situation objectively and making informed decisions.

To avoid emotional reactions:

- **Stay Grounded**: Keep your emotions in check and focus on facts rather than feelings.
- **Take a Step Back**: If you feel overwhelmed, take a break to regain perspective.
- **Seek Objective Opinions**: Consult others who can provide an unbiased view of the situation.

The Law of Big Words encompasses the deceptive tactic employed by individuals who lack genuine accomplishments but aim to project an illusion of greatness through grandiose claims. It is essential to discern the disparity between impressive assertions and actual achievements. By doing so, one can shield oneself from manipulation and embrace authenticity. It is crucial to bear in mind that genuine value and success are underscored by consistent actions and tangible accomplishments, rather than by grandiose proclamations.

CHAPTER XI

Law of Use and Throw

"Beware of those who charm you only to discard you—using you as a stepping stone before leaving you behind."

I. Introduction

The Law of Use and Throw is a behaviour pattern where individuals exploit others for their own gain and then discard them once their utility is exhausted. Unlike other manipulative tactics that may rely on ongoing deception or dominance, the Law of Use and Throw involves a more transactional and short-term approach.

At its core, this law involves creating a facade of friendliness or politeness to achieve a specific objective, such as getting help, favors, or resources. Once the goal is accomplished, the individual abruptly shifts their attention away from the person they exploited, effectively "throwing them away" once their purpose has been served. This behaviour is marked by a superficial charm that masks the true, utilitarian nature of the relationship.

People who use this law often exhibit a pattern of engaging warmly with others only when they need something. They might shower someone with attention and kindness when they are in need of a favor but will become indifferent or dismissive once that favor is granted. This creates a cycle of temporary engagement and manipulation, where individuals are valued only for what they can provide rather than for their intrinsic worth or mutual respect.

Understanding the Law of Use and Throw is crucial because it helps us recognize manipulative behaviours that can impact our relationships and emotional well-being. This law reveals how some individuals view relationships as mere transactions rather than genuine connections. By identifying these patterns, we can better protect ourselves from being exploited and ensure that our interactions are based on mutual respect and reciprocity.

In this chapter, we will explore the characteristics of the Law of Use and Throw, using real-life examples to illustrate how this behaviour manifests and affects those involved. We'll also discuss strategies for recognizing and safeguarding against such manipulative tactics to foster healthier and more authentic relationships.

II. *Characteristics of the Law of Use and Throw*

1. Initial Politeness and Charm

At the outset, individuals who practice the Law of Use and Throw often come across as exceptionally polite and charming. They know how to win people over by being friendly, attentive, and seemingly generous. This initial phase is designed to build trust and create a positive impression, making it easier for them to exploit others later. They might go out of their way to make others feel valued and appreciated, all the while having a hidden agenda.

1. Exploitation of Others

Once they've gained enough trust, these manipulators start exploiting their new acquaintances. They begin requesting favors, expecting assistance, or taking advantage of the relationship for their own benefit. This exploitation is often disguised as a need or genuine request, but the underlying intent is to use the other person's resources, time, or effort to achieve their own goals.

3. Sudden Withdrawal of Attention

After their purpose is served, individuals using this law abruptly withdraw their attention and interest. They suddenly become distant, unresponsive, or indifferent, as if the relationship never mattered. This sudden change is a clear sign that they've moved on to a new circle of people who can serve their next set of needs. The abrupt withdrawal leaves the other person feeling used and discarded.

4. Formation of New Circles

To continue their manipulative behaviour, these individuals constantly form new social circles. They repeat the cycle of gaining trust, exploiting, and discarding, all while maintaining a fresh set of connections to use. This continuous rotation allows them to leverage new people for their purposes without having to maintain genuine, long-term relationships.

5. Repeated Pattern of Use and Discard

The Law of Use and Throw is characterized by a repeated pattern of use and discard. It's not a one-time occurrence but a consistent strategy employed across different relationships and situations. By establishing a pattern, these individuals create a predictable cycle of exploitation, making it difficult for others to catch on until they've been hurt.

III. *Psychological Insights*

1. Manipulative Strategies

The primary strategy behind the Law of Use and Throw is manipulation. By presenting themselves as friendly and trustworthy, these individuals lower others' defenses, making it easier to extract what they need. The key is in the façade of politeness and charm, which masks their true intentions and manipulative tactics.

2. Emotional Impact on Others

The emotional impact on those who are used and discarded can be significant. People who fall victim to this law often feel hurt, betrayed, and undervalued. The abrupt shift from being valued to being ignored can lead to feelings of rejection and frustration. The emotional toll can affect self-esteem and trust in future relationships.

3. Human Tendency to Trust and Help

Human nature tends to be trusting and helpful. When someone appears genuine and in need, people are inclined to offer support and assistance. The Law of Use and Throw exploits this tendency by creating a false sense of trust and urgency, making it easy for manipulators to achieve their goals.

4. **Long-Term Effects on Relationships**

Over time, the repeated application of the Law of Use and Throw can lead to broader issues with trust and relationship dynamics. Individuals who frequently encounter this behaviour may become more guarded and cynical, impacting their ability to form genuine, meaningful connections in the future.

IV. *Personal Experience with Dabu*

To illustrate the Law of Use and Throw, let me share a personal experience involving my uncle, Dabu. His behaviour provides a clear example of how this manipulative tactic plays out in real life.

Dabu is known for his charm and apparent politeness, especially when he needs something. During family gatherings and special occasions, he presents himself as the epitome of goodwill and warmth. However, this façade quickly unravels once his needs are met.

One particular instance stands out. It was the birthday of Dabu's son, a significant event that required a substantial amount of preparation, including food for the guests. Dabu, keen on minimizing costs, asked his sister, my aunt, to help with the cooking. He approached her with a charming smile, complimented her, and expressed how much he appreciated her help. His demeanor was polite and considerate, making it seem like he genuinely valued her assistance.

My aunt, driven by familial affection and Dabu's apparent need, agreed to prepare the food for the event. She spent a considerable amount of time and effort to ensure everything was perfect for the birthday celebration. Dabu's gratitude during this period was palpable; he was courteous, thanking her repeatedly and acting as if he couldn't have managed the event without her.

But as soon as the celebration concluded, Dabu's attitude shifted drastically. He failed to acknowledge the favor once the event was over. The calls and messages of appreciation dwindled, and he didn't make any effort to stay in touch or reciprocate the kindness shown to him. It became apparent that once he had received what he needed, Dabu no longer had any interest in maintaining the relationship. He quickly moved on to form new connections, using others for his subsequent needs.

This pattern was not an isolated incident but rather a recurring behaviour. Each time a new event or need arose, Dabu would revert to his charming persona, exploit the goodwill of others, and then discard them when they were no longer useful. His actions demonstrated a clear cycle of using people and then moving on, leaving a trail of discarded relationships in his wake.

The impact on my aunt and others who experienced this behaviour was significant. They felt used and undervalued, realizing too late that their kindness had been exploited. Dabu's consistent use of the Law of Use and Throw served to highlight the manipulative nature of such individuals, who prioritize their own needs above genuine relationships and respect.

V. *Strategies for Dealing with Use and Throw Manipulation*

Understanding how to deal with individuals who practice the Law of Use and Throw is crucial for protecting yourself from being exploited. Here are some effective strategies to manage interactions with such manipulators:

1. Recognizing the Behaviour

The first step in addressing this manipulation is to recognize the behaviour patterns associated with the Law of Use and Throw. Be aware of individuals who display excessive charm and politeness only when they need something. Notice if their behaviour shifts abruptly once they have received what they wanted. Identifying these patterns early can help you avoid falling into their trap.

2. Setting Boundaries

Establishing clear boundaries is essential when dealing with people who use the Law of Use and Throw. It is important to communicate your limits and ensure that you are not taken advantage of. Politely but firmly set expectations about how you are willing to interact and what you are willing to offer. By setting boundaries, you can protect yourself from being used and discarded.

3. Evaluating the Relationship

Regularly evaluate the relationships in your life to determine if they are balanced and mutually beneficial. Be cautious of individuals who only reach out when they need something and show little interest in maintaining the relationship once their needs are met. Assess whether the relationship is based on genuine connection or if it is simply a cycle of use and discard.

4. Maintaining Awareness

Stay vigilant about changes in behaviour and patterns of interaction. If you notice that someone only engages with you when they need something, but becomes distant or unresponsive afterward, it's a sign of the Law of Use and Throw in action. Keeping track of these interactions can help you avoid becoming emotionally invested in relationships that are likely to end up being exploitative.

5. Building Genuine Relationships

Focus on building and nurturing relationships that are based on mutual respect and reciprocity. Invest your time and energy in connections where there is a genuine interest in maintaining the relationship and where both parties contribute equally. Genuine relationships are less likely to be affected by the manipulative tactics of the Law of Use and Throw.

By implementing these strategies, you can safeguard yourself from individuals who practice the Law of Use and Throw and foster more meaningful and respectful connections. Recognizing the signs of manipulation and setting clear boundaries are key to protecting yourself from being exploited.

The Law of Use and Throw is a manipulative tactic that leverages charm and politeness to exploit others before discarding them once their usefulness has been exhausted.

Through the experiences shared, particularly with Dabu, we've seen how this law operates in real-life situations, and how it can leave a trail of hurt and disappointment in its wake.

Understanding this behaviour is crucial for protecting oneself from falling victim to such manipulation. By recognizing the signs of exploitation, setting firm boundaries, and focusing on genuine relationships, you can shield yourself from being used and discarded.

While it can be disheartening to encounter individuals who employ the Law of Use and Throw, knowing how to identify and manage these relationships empowers you to maintain your integrity and self-respect. It's important to remember that not everyone operates under this law, and there are many people who value and nurture their relationships sincerely.

By being aware of these manipulative tactics and implementing the strategies outlined, you can foster healthier interactions and build connections that are based on mutual respect and genuine care. Your awareness and actions can not only protect you but also contribute to creating a more empathetic and authentic social environment.

In summary, the Law of Use and Throw highlights the importance of discernment in relationships. It serves as a reminder to be vigilant, set clear boundaries, and invest in relationships that are grounded in mutual respect and equality. Recognizing and addressing this law will help you navigate your social world with greater awareness and integrity.

CHAPTER XII

The real world

*"People who think the world is easy, in reality, it
is most difficult for them."*

As we reach the final chapter of the book "Fake Male", it's important to understand how to navigate the complexities of the real world. In today's world, people often try to dominate each other using the tactics discussed in the previous chapter. This applies to everyone, from local leaders to close friends to national figures. Everyone seems to be hungry for power, so even if you don't seek it, others may not perceive you the same way.

According to Darwin's theory, nature favours the most capable individuals for survival. To thrive in today's world, being powerful is essential. If you don't wish to manipulate others, be prepared to be manipulated, as that's the harsh reality. Even critical thinkers can be influenced through social media and by the influencers they follow

There's no straightforward escape from this reality. Once you understand the game of manipulation and seizing power, you will truly step into the real world, where you'll witness a blend of peace and brutality.

You might be confused as to why the discussion has shifted to being manipulated and powerful, given that the entire book revolves around identifying and dealing with manipulative individuals. The simple reason is **"survival of the fittest."** Understanding who seeks power and how to handle it will undoubtedly lead you to become a more powerful manipulator than them. Remember, there's nothing inherently wrong with manipulating others or seizing power.

"Manipulation is a pervasive force - either you manipulate or you get manipulated. The endgame is always power."